THE DBT SKILLS WORKBOOK FOR TEENS IS A FUN, ENGAGING AND GAMIFIED EXPERIENCE, PRECISELY WHAT KEEPS TODAY'S DISTRACTED TEENS MOTIVATED TO DO THE WORK. THAT IS ALREADY HALF THE BATTLE WON!

THIS BOOK SHOWS YOU HOW TO STAY IN CONTROL—BY BREATHING DEEPLY, SAYING POSITIVE THINGS TO YOURSELF, TALKING ABOUT YOUR FEELINGS, AND MORE. YOU'LL LEARN TO DEAL WITH ALL KIND OF FEELINGS, INCLUDING THE HARD ONES LIKE SADNESS, ANXIETY, OR EVEN FEAR.

Damed Art

WHEN A BIG FEELING COMES ALONG...
YOU CAN HANDLE IT!

Negative → Positive

My negative thought:

Evidence for my thought:

Evidence against my thought:

How can I reframe my negative thought to a more realistic one?

THOUGHT RECORD

A cognitive-behavioural strategy to capture and identify automatic negative thoughts.

EVENT
What happened?

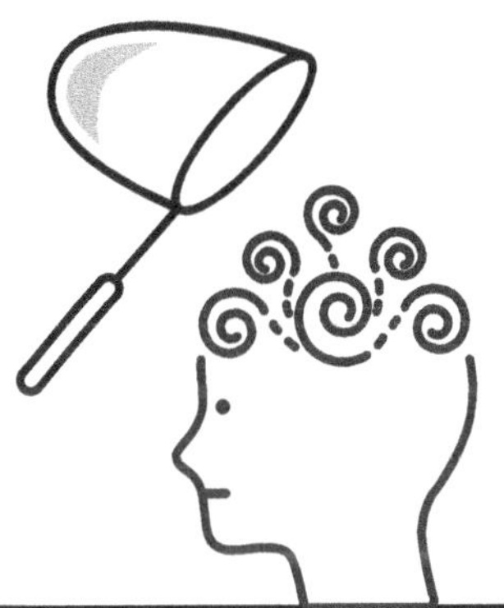

FEELINGS
How did it make me feel?

THOUGHTS
What was I telling myself when the event was happening?

BEHAVIOUR
What was my response to the situation?

SUPPORTIVE EVIDENCE
Why is my thought true?

NON-SUPPORTIVE EVIDENCE
Why might my thought not be true?

PROBLEM DISCOVERY
The Five Ps Case Formulation

Helping me make sense of a current difficulty

Presenting Problem: the feelings, thoughts and behaviours that are causing me concern:

Predisposing Factors:

Factors that predisposed me or made me vulnerable to the problem:

Precipitating Factors:

Current triggers that contribute to the problem:

Perpetuating Factors: Things that are keeping the problem going:

Protective Factors: The good things in my life that are a source of strength:

5-4-3-2-1

GROUNDING TECHNIQUE

A calming technique that connects you with the present by exploring the five senses.

Instructions: Sitting or standing, take a deep breath in, and complete the following questions.

5
5 things you can see

4
4 things you can touch

3
3 things you can hear

2
2 things you can smell

1
1 thing you can taste

THOUGHT CLOUDS

In the clouds, write words to describe your thoughts and feelings.

MANAGING EMOTIONS

Interview a classmate for this activity. Listen to the story carefully and take down notes. Then, answer the questions below.

When was the last time he or she wanted something but did not get it? It may be something they longed for or an event that did not happen.

1.) What do you think your classmate felt during that time? Write at least four emotions you can associate with the story shared to you.

2.) What do you think your classmate could have said to himself or herself to process those emotions? Write two sentences of positive self-talk.

3.) What do you think your classmate should have actively done (or already did) to cope with those emotions? List three activities you noted or would recommend.

EMOTIONS!

Name: _________________________   Date: _________________________

My Visual Journal

Read the prompts below and respond by filling each space
provided with images and words that come into mind.

The best things that happened today:	Things I wish I can change about today:
I am proud of myself today because...	I think I still need to work on....

HELLO FRIENDS!

FEELING FACES

Draw the expressions on each of the faces to match the feelings:

My Daily Emotions Log

Choose two words from the list to describe how you feel today. Can't find your emotions there? Feel free to use other words.

I think these feelings are:

○ both positive   ○ positive and negative
○ negative and positive   ○ both negative

I feel this way because _______________________

____

____

____

____

What can cheer you up or help you stay happy today? Draw them below.

EMOTIONS LIST

angry
annoyed
anxious
ashamed
awkward
brave
calm
cheerful
chill
confused
discouraged
disgusted
distracted
embarrassed
excited
friendly
guilty
happy
hopeful
jealous
lonely
loved
nervous
offended
scared
thoughtful
tired
uncomfortable
unsure
worried

MY ULTIMATE COPING PLAYLIST

We go through different positive and negative emotions everyday. It is okay to have all those feelings but we must also find ways to cope.

Fill each box with the title of songs (and their artist) that you think fit the descriptions provided.

FOR AMUSEMENT

a song that gets stuck in my head

a song I know all the words to

a song from my favorite movie or tv series

TO UPLIFT

a song I associate to freedom

a song that gives me energy

a song I'd like to wake me up

FOR DIVERSION

a song that makes me feel safe

a song that helps me think positively

a song that inspires me

TO DISCHARGE

a song for when you get anxious worried

a song for when you get angry or annoyed

a song for when you feel lonely or afraid

FOR STRONG EMOTIONS

a song that reminds you of a good memory

a song that makes you think of a loved one

a song to remind you that you are loved

Mood Match

Can you tell the color of the feelings below?
Color the word box of each picture based on
the mood thermometer.

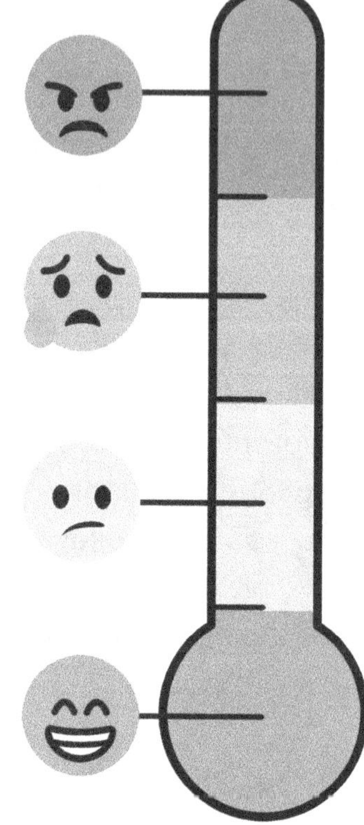

happy

sad

hurt

shy

loved

tired

silly

scared

BACK TO SCHOOL!

Ultimate Coping Playlist

Make the perfect coping playlist for you by giving this challenge a try

Entertainment	A song that stays stuck in your head when you hear it.	A song you know all the words to.	Your favorite song from a movie.
Revival	A song that represents freedom	A song that you'd listen to fall asleep.	A song that makes you feel pumped up.
Strong Sensation	A song that reminds you of a good memory.	A song that reminds you of someone you care about	A song that reminds you of someone who cares about you
Diversion	A song that makes you feel safe.	A song you find inspirational.	Your go to positivity song.
Discharge	A song that matches your vibe you get when you feel anxious or worried.	A song that matches your vibe when you feel annoyed or angry.	A song that matches your vibe when you feel sad or afraid.

Name: Date:

My Week of Emotions

Our emotions can be divided into four zones: blue, green, yellow, and red.   We always try to stay or go back to the green zone and avoid the red zone.

Fill out the calendar below for an overview of the zones you go through in a week.

SUNDAY

Today I felt:

To stay in the green zone, I tried to:

MONDAY

Today I felt:

To stay in the green zone, I tried to:

TUESDAY

Today I felt:

To stay in the green zone, I tried to:

WEDNESDAY

Today I felt:

To stay in the green zone, I tried to:

THURSDAY

Today I felt:

To stay in the green zone, I tried to:

FRIDAY

Today I felt:

To stay in the green zone, I tried to:

SATURDAY

Today I felt:

To stay in the green zone, I tried to:

ZONES OF REGULATION

Low energy and motivation to participate	Attentive and feeling positive overall	Uncomfortable and needs to focus	Full of negative emotions and may react harshly

BACK TO SCHOOL EMOJIS

Cut out an emoji from page two to describe your emotions about coming back to school and then write a paragraph explaining your choice.

NAME

DATE

SECTION

SCORE

WHAT AM I SCARED OF?

CAN YOU CLEARLY CONVEY YOUR FEARS?

Immerse in your emotions and explain your biggest fear. Is it dying alone or being unsuccessful in your career? Or is it simply public speaking or a fear of rejection? Whatever it is, write about your greatest fear in no more than 100 words.

Emotions

Draw the expressions on the faces to match the emotion.

MANDALA ADULT COLORING PAGE

MANDALA ADULT COLORING PAGE

MANDALA ADULT COLORING PAGE

MANDALA ADULT COLORING PAGE

 # EMERGENCY 

What do I say?

Scenario: You've discovered your carer has collapsed. There is no one at home except you. Where would you look to find a phone to call for help?

____

What number do you call?   ____________________________________

Complete the following:

"Hello, this is emergency services, what is your emergency?"

____

____

____

____

"What is your name?"   ____________________________________

"Is anybody else at home?"   ____________________________________

"We will send someone over to help you. What is your address?"

____

____

____

"You're doing a great job. Stay calm and someone will be with you soon".

Essay Writing Exercise

Write an essay based on this prompt:

Think back to a time when you accidentally broke something at home. How did you feel? What happened? Share your thoughts and emotions at the time and what happened afterwards.

____

____

____

____

____

____

____

____

____

____

____

____

____

____

____

____

____

____

Resilience STRATEGIES

Write strategies that you have used in the past, or could use in the future to help you successfully overcome a challenge.

My Protective Factors

Protective factors help you be resilient when faced with challenges. Fill in the below areas to help identify strengths in your life.

Social Support

List two people in your life that you can talk to about your problems.

Skills

Describe at least one thing you are good at, or have knowledge on.

Coping Strategies

Describe a time when you've overcome a challenge.

Personal Identity

Describe something you are proud of, relating to your personal identity.

Community

List any interest activities you are engaged in.

Conjunctions

Word that connect sentences, phrases or ideas together.

Instructions: Underline the conjunctions in the following sentences:

- I am going to the zoo and will see a giraffe.

- I like carrots, but I like cucumbers more.

- He went for a bike ride as it was a sunny day.

- I would like a dog for taking on walks.

- Mum said I can have ice cream or custard for dessert.

- Neither mum nor dad heard the loud bang in the night.

Instructions: Write sentences using the following conjunctions:

or: ____

____

____

yet: ____

____

____

so: ____

____

____

Negative → Positive

My negative thought:

Evidence for my thought:

Evidence against my thought:

How can I reframe my negative thought to a more realistic one?

KINDNESS IS CONTAGIOUS

It feels so good when someone says something nice to you.. But often, we forget to tell someone when we think they have done a great job, or when we admire a quality in them. Choose four people in your class to write a kind, specific message to. Try to write one for someone who isn't in your immediate friendship group.

Life GOALS

In the spaces below, brainstorm all the big things you'd like to achieve over your lifetime

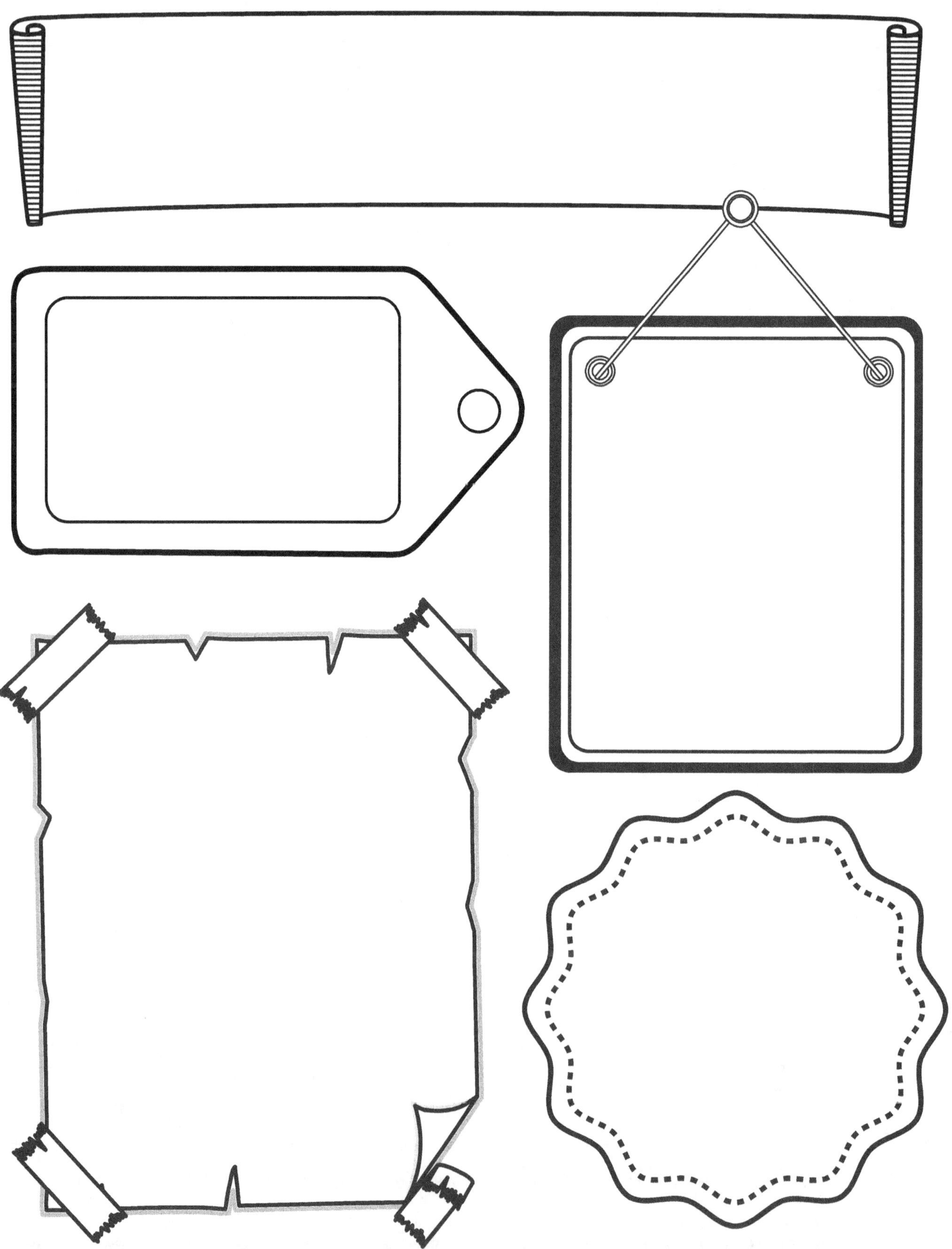

SELF *love*

IN THE SPACES BELOW, LIST ALL THE WAYS YOU CAN SHOW
LOVE AND APPRECIATION TO YOURSELF

THANKSGIVING
COUNT

Instructions: Count each item, then tally them into the boxes below:

What does it mean to be mindful?

____

____

____

____

____

____

How can you practice being mindful every day?

____

____

____

____

____

____

____

____

THE FIVE SENSES

H	E	A	R	I	N	G	S	S	S	S
L	A	O	L	I	N	G	M	N	I	D
L	R	A	N	G	M	F	E	B	G	R
E	S	I	A	T	O	E	L	S	H	O
M	K	R	T	S	T	U	L	N	T	T
S	S	E	A	S	T	G	T	E	S	P
T	E	A	F	Q	E	N	E	Y	L	E
B	R	A	I	N	R	O	U	E	L	C
E	N	O	S	E	N	T	T	S	E	E
M	O	S	E	N	S	E	S	A	C	R
T	O	U	C	H	E	D	L	R	O	W

Instructions: Find the <u>underlined</u> words in the above find-a-word.

We experience the <u>world</u> through our <u>five</u> <u>senses</u>. These senses send information to our <u>brain</u> via <u>receptor</u> <u>cells.</u> The five senses are: <u>hearing</u>, <u>sight</u>, <u>smell</u>, <u>taste</u> and <u>touch</u>. We use our <u>ears</u> to hear, <u>eyes</u> to see, <u>nose</u> to smell, <u>skin</u> to touch and both our nose and <u>tongue</u> to taste.

1.

2.

Mandala Coloring

Mandala Coloring

Mandala Coloring

Mandala Coloring

A PEEK INSIDE MY MIND

Draw your face here, and then lift the fold to reveal your thoughts!

My name is

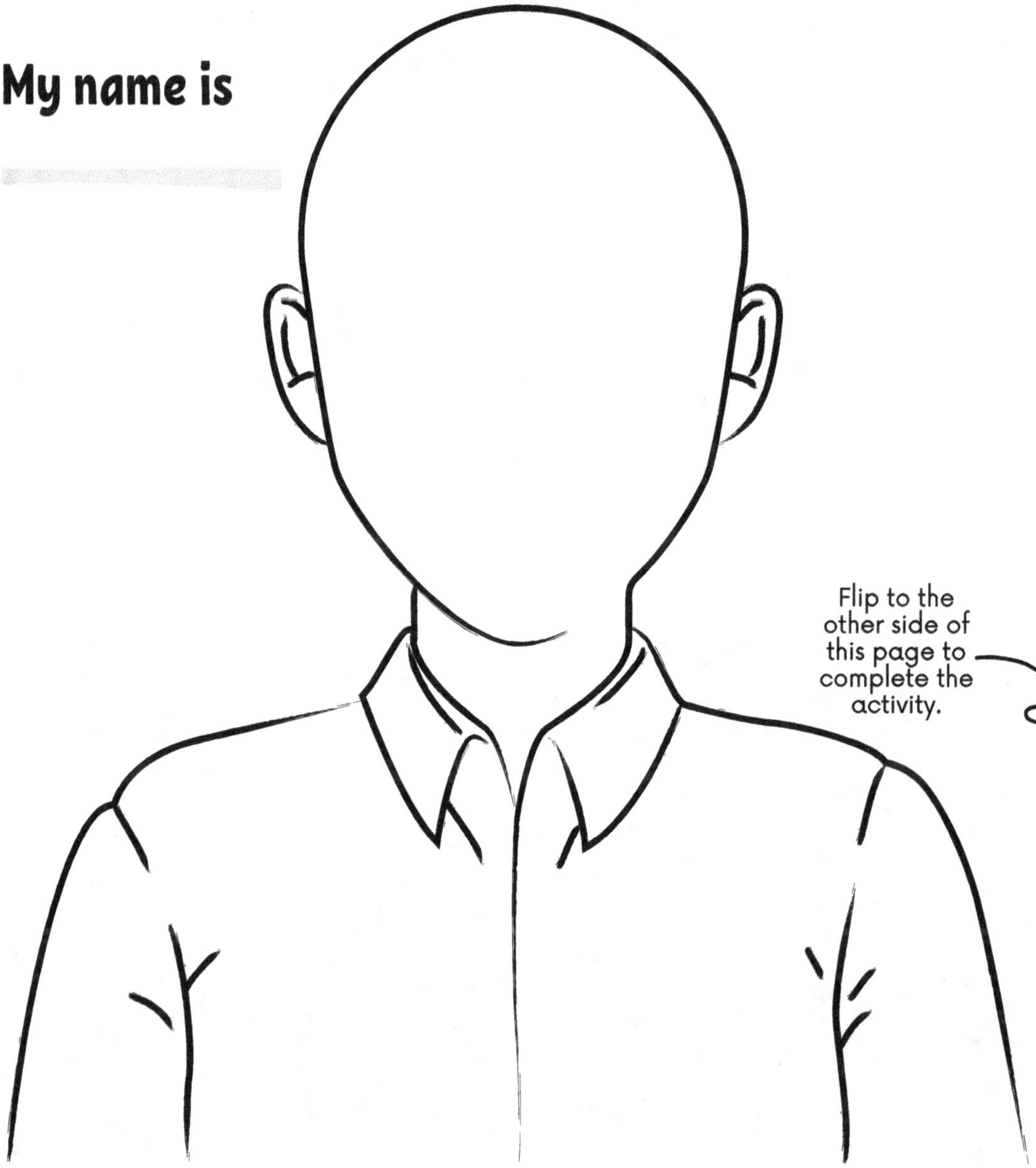

Flip to the other side of this page to complete the activity.

A PEEK INSIDE MY MIND

In these clouds, write down all of your thoughts and feelings that are having.
They can be happy thoughts, sad thoughts, worried thoughts, excited thoughts!

WHAT MAKES ME HAPPY 😄

Write a well constructed paragraph using the writing prompt below.

When I'm happy, _______________________________

ALL ABOUT ME

MY PORTRAIT

____
AGE

____
MY FAVORITE FOOD

____
MY LEAST FAVORITE FOOD

____
MY TEACHER

____
MY PETS

____
MY FAVORITE SONG

____
MY BEST FRIEND

____
WHAT MAKES ME HAPPY

____
WHAT MAKES ME SAD

ALL ABOUT ME!

My name is _______________________

I am __________ years old.

I live in ___________________________

I am excited about _______________
____
____

Me

My Favorite Activities

My Favorite Foods

My Favorite Books

My Favorite Games

HAPPY TEETH

Find and color the same two teeth

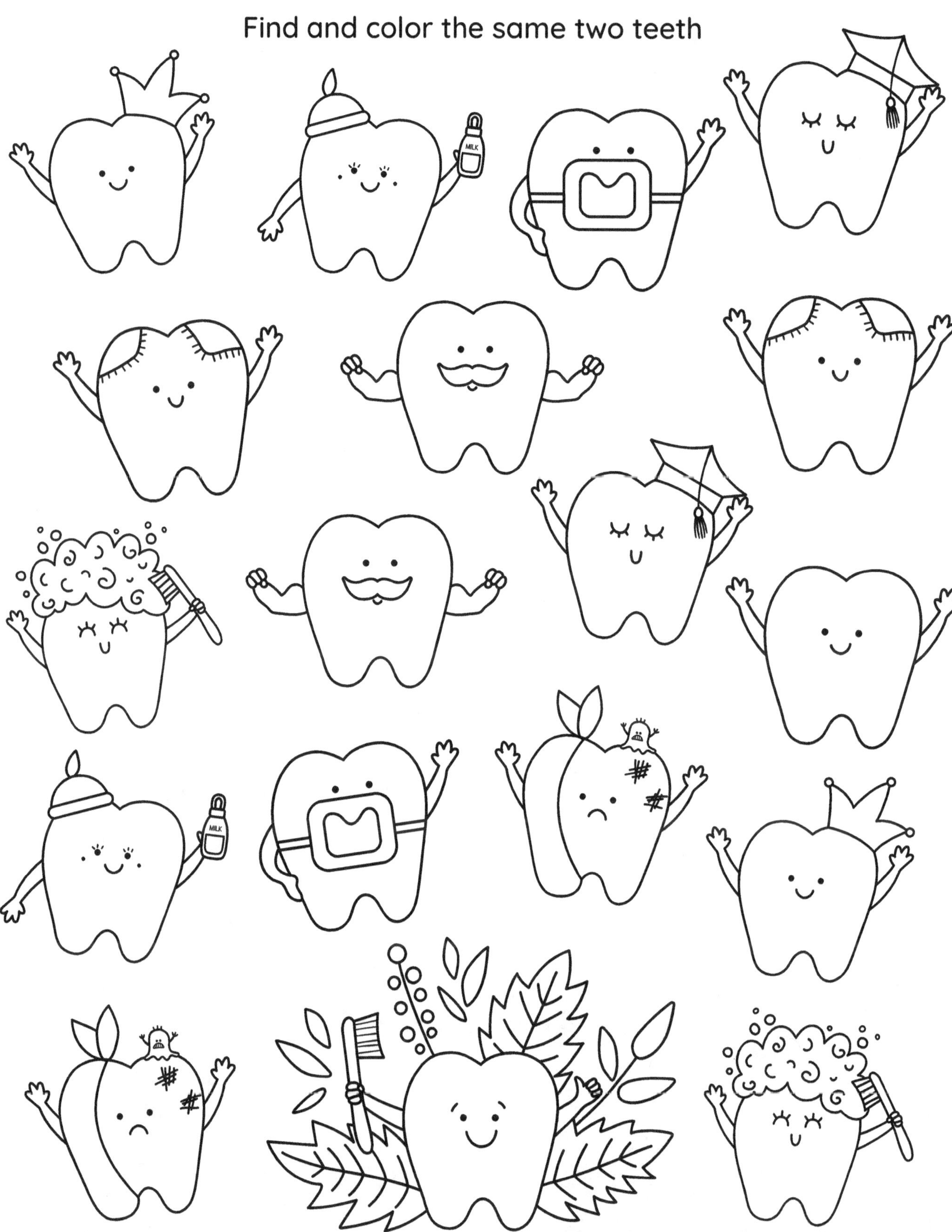

Lockdown REFLECTION

How I feel about returning to the classroom

The main reason for my rating

____
____
____

I'm most excited about

____
____
____
____

I'm most nervous about

____
____
____
____

A good thing about lockdown was

____
____

Body Scan

Close your eyes. Take a deep breath in through your nose, and out through your mouth. Starting with the top of your head, become aware of how your body feels. Slowly move down your body, noticing how each body part feels, down to your toes. Make a note of any areas of discomfort on the body below. Draw a face on the person to represent how you are currently feeling.

Body Scan

Close your eyes. Take a deep breath in through your nose, and out through your mouth. Starting with the top of your head, become aware of how your body feels. Slowly move down your body, noticing how each body part feels, down to your toes. Make a note of any areas of discomfort on the body below. Draw a face on the person to represent how you are currently feeling.

WHAT'S IN MY HEAD?

Write or draw all the thoughts you have on your mind.

WHAT'S IN MY HEAD?

Write or draw all the thoughts you have on your mind.

5-4-3-2-1
GROUNDING TECHNIQUE

A calming technique that connects you with the present by exploring the five senses.

Instructions: Sitting or standing, take a deep breath in, and complete the following questions.

BUTTERFLIES

THOUGHT RECORD

A cognitive-behavioural strategy to capture and identify automatic negative thoughts.

EVENT
What happened?

FEELINGS
How did it make me feel?

THOUGHTS
What was I telling myself when the event was happening?

BEHAVIOUR
What was my response to the situation?

SUPPORTIVE EVIDENCE
Why is my thought true?

NON-SUPPORTIVE EVIDENCE
Why might my thought not be true?

M I N D F U L *Reflections*

Use your 5 senses to explore each item, writing down your reflections.

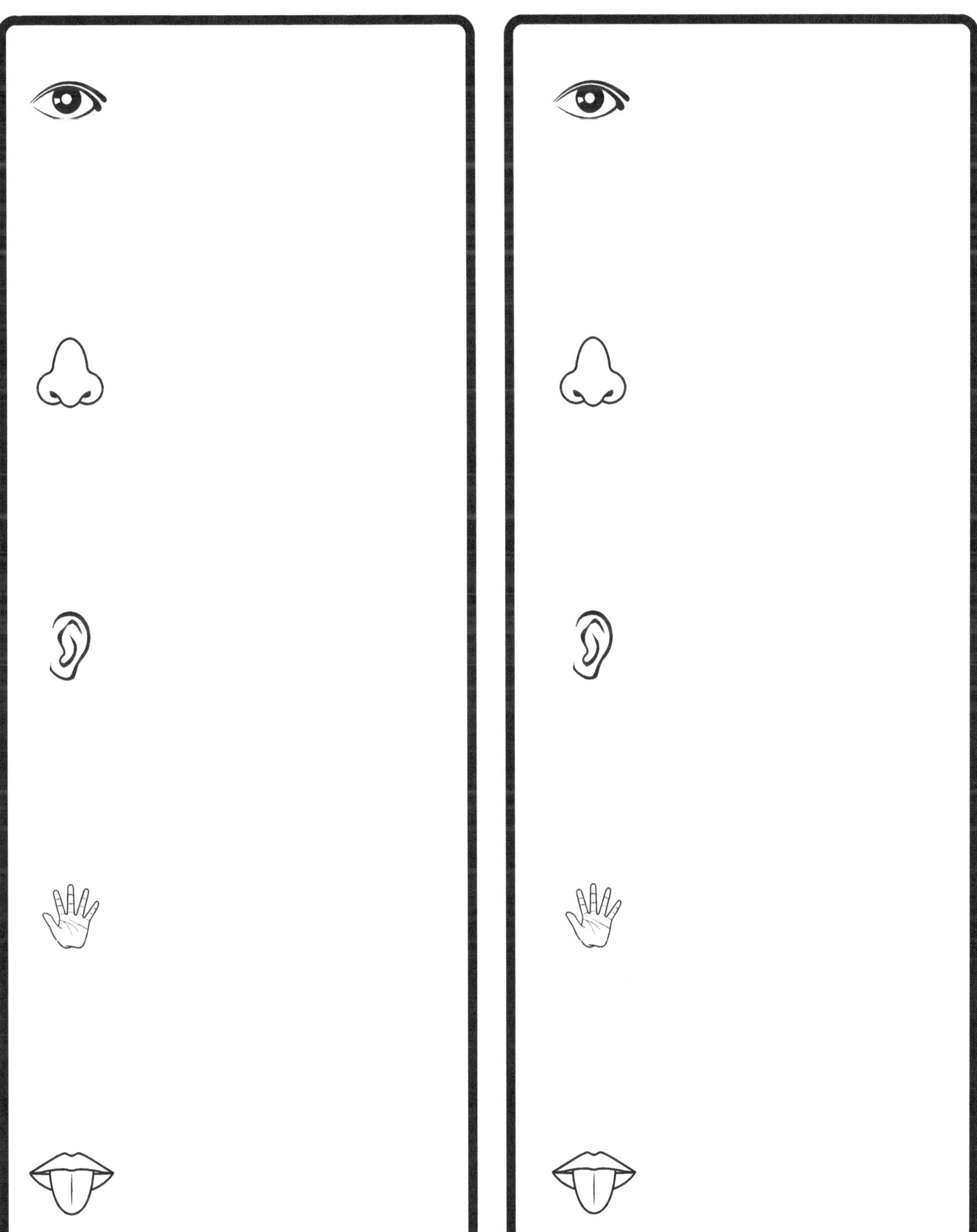

FEAR CRUSHER

MY GOAL:

ANXIETY-PRODUCING SITUATION

Mandala Coloring

Mandala Coloring

Mandala Coloring

POSITIVE GROWTH MINDSET

You are having some friendship problems with some classmates and it's beginning to interfere with your studies. What action should you take?

____

____

____

____

____

____

____

____

____

a strong
LEADER
is

My Favorite Art Movement

Among the different art movements we spoke about in class, which one was the most interesting for you?

Choose 3 paintings from that art movement and paste them onto the boxes below.

Provide 4 facts about this art movement. Each fact should be 1-3 sentences.

Why do you think people liked this art movement? What do you like about it?

MY MASTERPIECE

A planning worksheet for your final project

I'M GOING TO CREATE A:

Traditional Painting

☐ Digital Artwork

☐ Sculpture

☐

☐ Collage

☐ Other:

I'LL BE GETTING MY INSPIRATION FROM:

(an artist, a concept, a personal experience, another culture, etc.)

THE ELEMENTS AND PRINCIPLES THAT I'LL HIGHLIGHT ARE:

Encircle 4-5 items from the list:

line	form	color	space	variety
shape	value	texture	unity	rhythm
pattern	emphasis	balance	proportion	

HERE'S AN INITIAL SKETCH OF MY MASTERPIECE:

Gratitude Banner

Directions: Complete the thought with a drawing or words. Cut out and turn for hanging in the classroom.

Name: Date:

Nursery Art

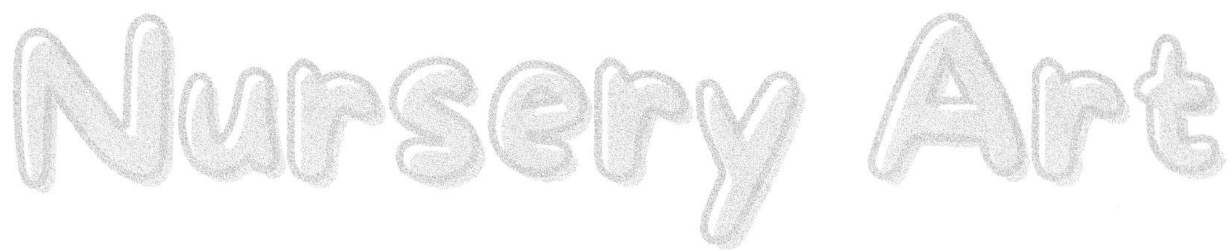

Practice math and your drawing skills with this beautiful nursery art exercise. Draw the other side.

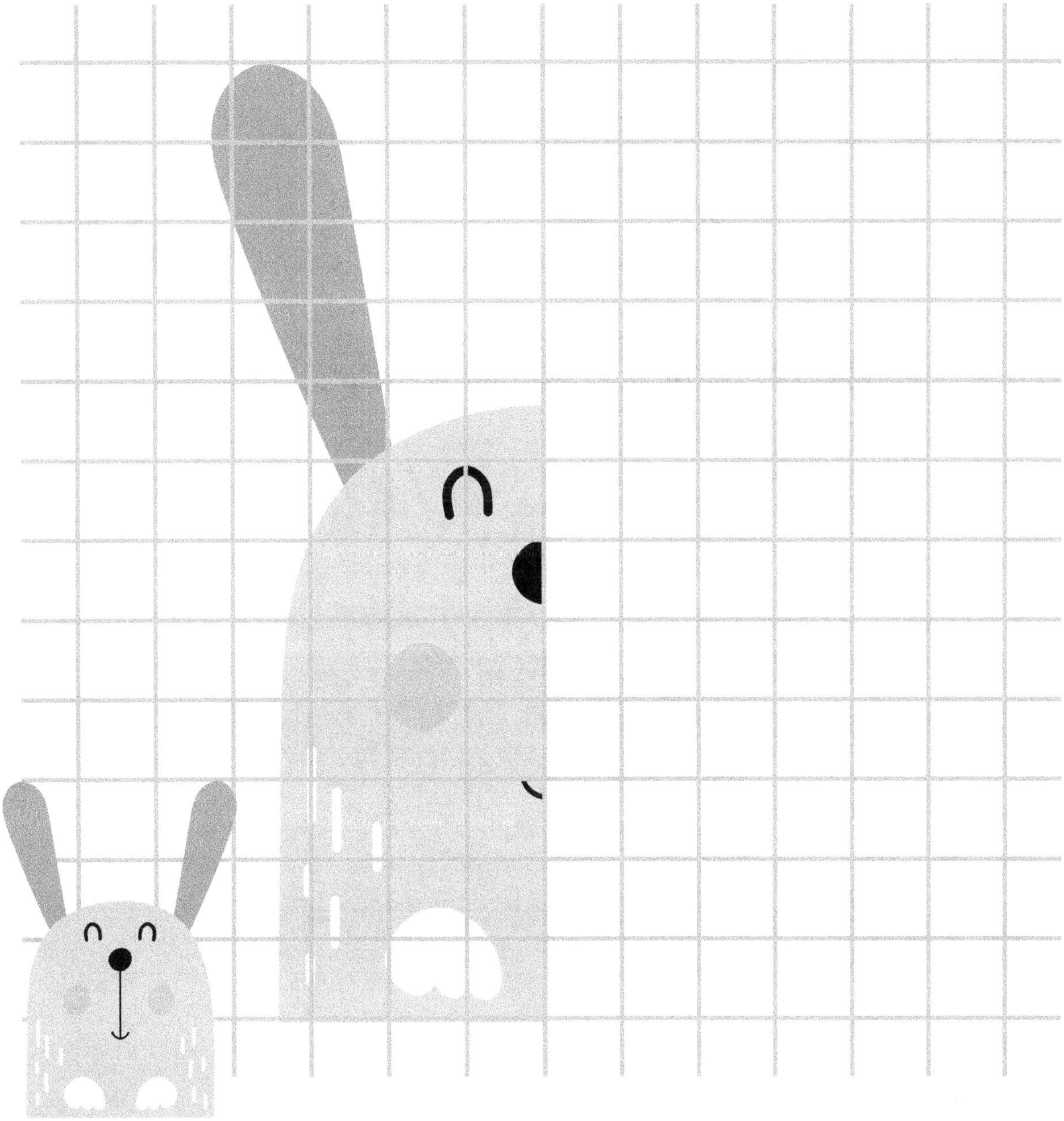

Nursery Art

Practice math and your drawing skills with this
beautiful nursery art exercise. Draw the other side.

Nursery Art

Practice math and your drawing skills with this beautiful nursery art exercise. Draw the other side.

MAZE GAME

Can you help mama bird to find the way?

GREATER OR LESS THAN

Compare the numbers and write <, >, or =

10 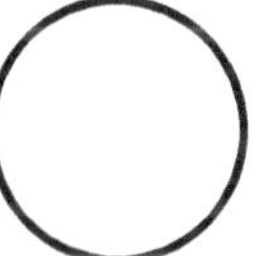 8	1  10
6  7	3  3
5 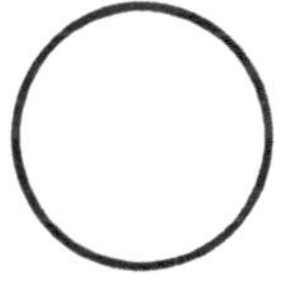 5	0  8
3 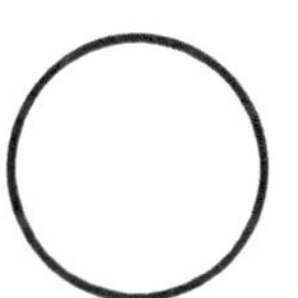 9	7 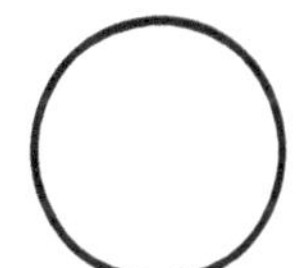 9
4 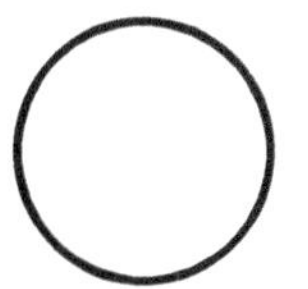 2	6 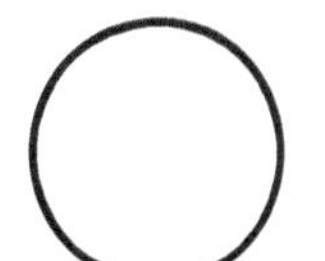 4

Number Values

Color the number that has the bigger value

Patterns

Look at the shapes and cross out the one that would come next to complete the pattern.

THE HUMAN BODY

H	E	A	R	I	N	R	E	T	A	W
L	H	U	M	A	N	N	I	A	R	B
L	R	E	A	G	M	A	C	B	G	O
E	S	I	A	T	O	L	O	S	H	N
M	E	R	H	R	T	I	N	N	T	E
S	N	E	I	D	T	V	T	E	S	S
S	S	A	N	O	E	E	R	Y	L	E
L	E	A	E	O	R	O	O	E	L	C
L	S	O	S	L	N	T	L	O	E	E
E	O	R	G	B	A	N	S	A	B	R
C	O	U	C	S	E	U	S	S	I	T

Instructions: Find the underlined words in the above find-a-word.

The human body is a complex machine. It is made up of cells, organs and tissues. Around 60% of the body is water. A baby is born with 270 bones, and this decreases to 206 by adulthood. The brain is the control centre and takes in information from the five senses (sight, hearing, smell, taste and touch). The heart pumps blood around the body, keeping it alive.

THE FIVE SENSES

H	E	A	R	I	N	G	S	S	S	S
L	A	O	L	I	N	G	M	N	I	D
L	R	A	N	G	M	F	E	B	G	R
E	S	I	A	T	O	E	L	S	H	O
M	K	R	T	S	T	U	L	N	T	T
S	S	E	A	S	T	G	T	E	S	P
T	E	A	F	Q	E	N	E	Y	L	E
B	R	A	I	N	R	O	U	E	L	C
E	N	O	S	E	N	T	T	S	E	E
M	O	S	E	N	S	E	S	A	C	R
T	O	U	C	H	E	D	L	R	O	W

Instructions: Find the underlined words in the above find-a-word.

We experience the world through our five senses. These senses send information to our brain via receptor cells. The five senses are: hearing, sight, smell, taste and touch. We use our ears to hear, eyes to see, nose to smell, skin to touch and both our nose and tongue to taste.

HONEST

What does it mean to be honest?

____

____

____

____

____

List three good things that can come from telling the truth:

RESPONSIBLE

What does it mean to be responsible?

____

____

____

____

____

List all the activities you are personally responsible for doing after you get home from school in the afternoon (eg unpack your school bag):

COURAGE

What does it mean to be courageous?

____

____

____

____

____

Describe a time when you had to be brave, and how you
felt before, during and after:

RESILIENT

What does it mean to be resilient?

____

____

____

____

____

List three strategies that have helped you be resilient in the past:

1

2

3

PATIENT

Write your own definition for what being patient means:

____

____

____

____

____

The girls have been waiting a long time for their dad to pick them up. Suggest some activities they can do to pass the time patiently:

RESPECT

Write your own definition for respect:

____

____

____

____

____

Fill in the speech bubbles to demonstrate a respectful conversation:

Name: Date:

KNOCK-KNOCK!

ANYONE HOME?

Draw and label all the creatures that call the ocean home:

KNOCK-KNOCK!

ANYONE HOME?

Draw and label all the creatures that call a tree home:

<table>
<tr><td>Name</td><td>Grade & Section</td><td>Teacher</td><td>Date</td></tr>
</table>

Solar System Crossword

Answer the questions below by filling in the blanks in the puzzle.

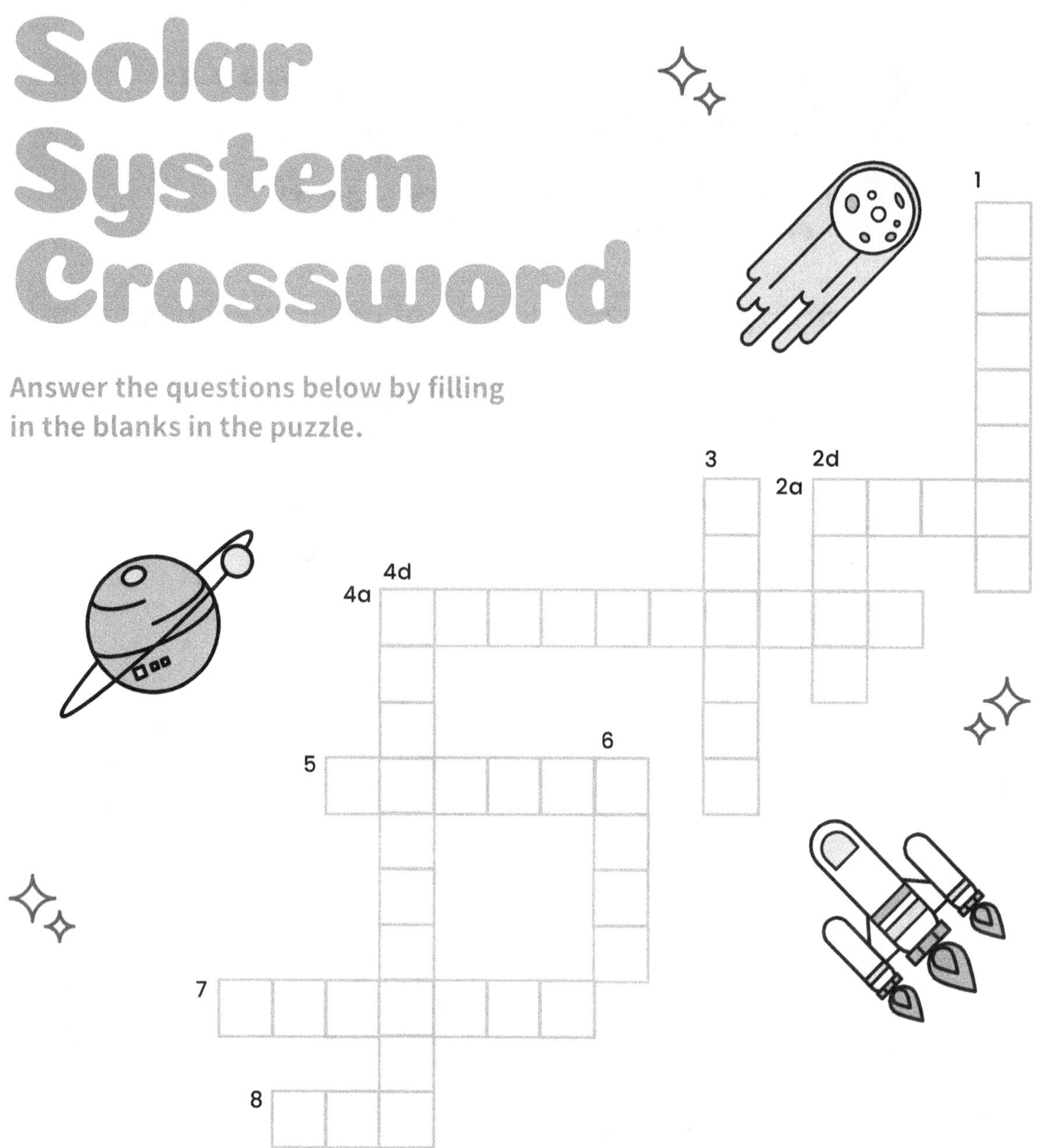

ACROSS

- 2a - The planet with the moons Phobos & Deimos.
- 4a - What the moon's light is caused by?
- 5 - Objects that are commonly made of snow, ice, and dust, and can be found moving around outer space.
- 7 - The planet famous for its red spot.
- 8 - The center of our solar system.

DOWN

- 1 - What occurs when one heavenly body (moon or planet) moves into the shadow of another?
- 2d - This is Earth's satellite.
- 3 - The planet that has the most number of rings.
- 4d - One turn around the sun that equals 365 days is called?
- 6 - What is the sun?

PUZZLE *fun*

Decorate your puzzle with your favorite memory from your vacation. Then cut out your puzzle and have a friend solve it!

FIND YOUR INNER PIECE
Mindful colouring puzzle

Instructions: Colour in the picture, then cut around the pieces. Ask a friend or family member if they can put your puzzle back together.

THANKSGIVING JIGSAW

Instructions: Colour in the picture, then cut around the pieces. Ask a friend or family member if they can put your puzzle back together.

Geography of Thanksgiving

What better way to learn about Thanksgiving than through history and geography?
Fill in the missing word/s in each statement. Some letters have been provided as
hints. Then, find and cross out each word in the word search box.

1. The first recorded Thanksgiving in the ________________________________ was in 1621.

2. In 1620, the merchant ship called the Mayflower landed on the shores of ____________.

3. The most known and the world's biggest annual Thanksgiving parade is held every year in ________________City.

4. The pilgrims who landed in the shores of North America came from ________________.

5. ____________________ is the leading producer of cranberries in the US.

6. Two of the towns in the United States named "Turkey" are found in the states of ________ and __________.

U	R	A	B	B	I	T	W	P	S	X	F	D	Z	O	Y
S	P	R	I	N	G	L	E	F	A	M	I	L	Y	A	B
D	C	C	Z	A	P	R	I	L	U	Z	N	D	M	K	C
B	G	R	H	Y	C	D	A	F	F	O	D	I	L	B	H
A	C	U	E	O	E	E	Z	P	U	G	B	H	R	E	I
S	Z	E	G	M	C	C	H	I	W	V	B	F	R	O	C
K	D	S	G	V	F	O	Y	A	D	Q	U	O	F	D	K
E	H	U	S	Q	X	R	L	P	P	O	N	X	Z	O	Y
T	G	N	B	O	I	A	E	A	S	P	N	D	L	F	B
R	W	D	J	C	Y	T	W	K	T	F	Y	F	K	H	O
C	P	A	R	A	D	E	W	P	E	E	X	J	Z	A	N
E	W	Y	O	K	I	X	T	R	A	D	I	T	I	O	N
Q	J	E	A	S	T	E	R	P	V	S	K	P	J	A	E
T	U	L	I	P	S	G	D	I	H	U	N	T	P	Y	T

April	Tradition	Easter	Happy	Tulips
Daffodil	Spring	Bunny	Bonnet	Decorate
Find	Eggs	Chocolate	Sunday	Parade
Basket	Rabbit	Chick	Hunt	Family

SPOT THE DIFFERENCE
COLORING SHEET

CHRISTMAS
CONNECT-THE-DOTS

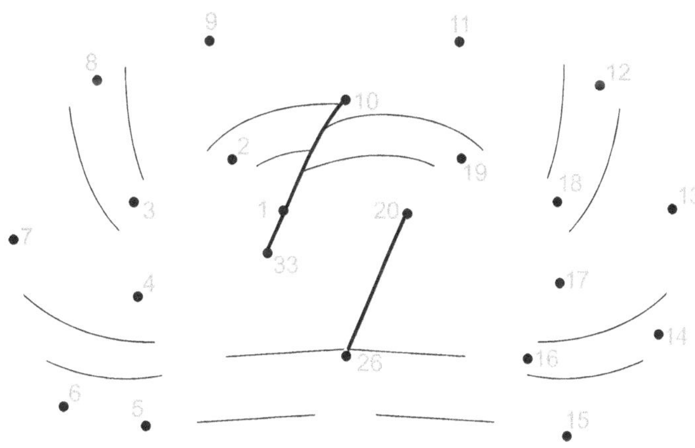

GRAMMAR

Instructions: Use the key below to colour the puzzle pieces:

Nouns: Blue   Verbs: Red   Adjectives: Green   Adverbs: Orange

man	dance	dog	cried	bird	walk
skip	tall	graceful	fat	long	door
toes	hard	six	long	angry	think
wash	happy	always	funny	soon	table
Peacock	next	wrinkly	constantly	red	drinking
climb	Tom	play	London	sit	pencil

BACK TO SCHOOL WORD SEARCH

Circle words in the puzzle below

B	U	S	N	B	M	A	T	H
E	R	E	C	E	S	S	E	D
S	C	U	D	L	R	K	A	F
D	C	N	E	L	E	H	C	R
E	E	H	A	R	A	F	H	I
T	R	S	O	D	D	U	E	E
C	F	N	K	O	A	N	R	N
L	U	N	C	H	L	P	G	D
C	N	O	C	G	A	M	E	S

bus	school	recess	bell
desk	games	lunch	read
friends	teacher	fun	math

VALENTINE'S DAY WORD SEARCH

Circle words in the puzzle below

```
B L O V E P O L T
O S B A C U P I D
W C U L W C L K F
B A S E U E H E R
L N W N R D E N I
O D E T O C A R E
C Y E I C A R D N
K U T N V C T R D
P I N E A R R O W
```

love	arrow	care	valentine
sweet	bow	friend	heart
like	candy	card	cupid